THE PERSEVERANCE MARS ROVER

DONNA REYNOLDS

PowerKiDS
press

Published in 2025 by The Rosen Publishing Group, Inc.
2544 Clinton Street, Buffalo, NY 14224

First Edition

Editor: Jennifer Lombardo
Book Design: Rachel Rising

Photo Credits: Cover, p. 14 Anterovium/Shutterstock.com; cover, pp. 1, 3–32 KK.KICKIN/Shutterstock.com; p. 4 Fordelse Stock/Shutterstock.com; p. 5 https://en.m.wikipedia.org/wiki/File:Mars_t%C3%A9lescope.jpg; p. 7 awstoys/Shutterstock.com; p. 9 Vivvi Smak/Shutterstock.com; p.11 NASA/JPL-Caltech/MSSS; p. 13 https://commons.m.wikimedia.org/wiki/File:Curiosity_rover_selfie_at_Mont_Mercou_Sol_3070_(53677088587).jpg; p. 15 NASA/JPL-Caltech/ASU; p. 16 https://commons.wikimedia.org/wiki/File:PIA24202-MarsPerseveranceRover-Moxie-Testing-20210119.jpg; pp.17, 19, 20, 21, 25, 29 NASA/JPL-Caltech; pp. 18, 26 Artsiom P/Shutterstock.com; p. 22 https://en.m.wikipedia.org/wiki/File:Perseverance%27s_First_Full-Color_Look_at_Mars.png; p. 23 penofoto/Shutterstock.com; p. 24 mineral vision/Shutterstock.com; p. 27 https://en.wikipedia.org/wiki/File:Plutonium_pellet.jpg; p. 28 elRoce/Shutterstock.com.

Library of Congress Cataloging-in-Publication Data
Names: Reynolds, Donna, 1976-.
Title: The Perseverance Mars rover / Donna Reynolds.
Description: Buffalo, NY : PowerKids Press, 2025. | Series: Mission control | Includes glossary and index.
Identifiers: ISBN 9781499449907 (pbk.) | ISBN 9781499449914 (library bound) | ISBN 9781499449921 (ebook)
Subjects: LCSH: Perseverance (Spacecraft)--Juvenile literature. | Roving vehicles (Astronautics)--Juvenile literature. | Mars (Planet)--Exploration--Juvenile literature.
Classification: LCC TL475 .R49 2025 | DDC 629.295--dc23

Manufactured in the United States of America

Some of the images in this book illustrate individuals who are models. The depictions do not imply actual situations or events.

CPSIA Compliance Information: Batch #CWPK25. For further information contact Rosen Publishing at 1-800-237-9932.

Find us on 

CONTENTS

FOCUSING ON MARS

Humans have been fascinated with Mars for thousands of years. Although Mars is not particularly special as far as planets go, it was given higher status by the fact that early astronomers believed it could be home to other living things. Humans became captivated by the idea that we were not alone in our solar system.

Although it has been proven that there is no advanced civilization on Mars, scientists and science fans alike still want to know more about this planet. Ever since space exploration became possible, astronomers have done their best to get close to Mars. Early efforts generally did not go well, but scientists did not give up. Today, there are multiple machines on Mars, gathering all kinds of information.

A HISTORY OF MISTAKES

Early astronomers made many wrong guesses about what they were seeing on Mars. For example, in 1895, a man named Percival Lowell drew a map of what he could see through his telescope. On the map, he drew and labeled **canals**, saying that they had been dug by intelligent beings. Although these ideas were later proven to be false, our fascination with Mars has never gone away.

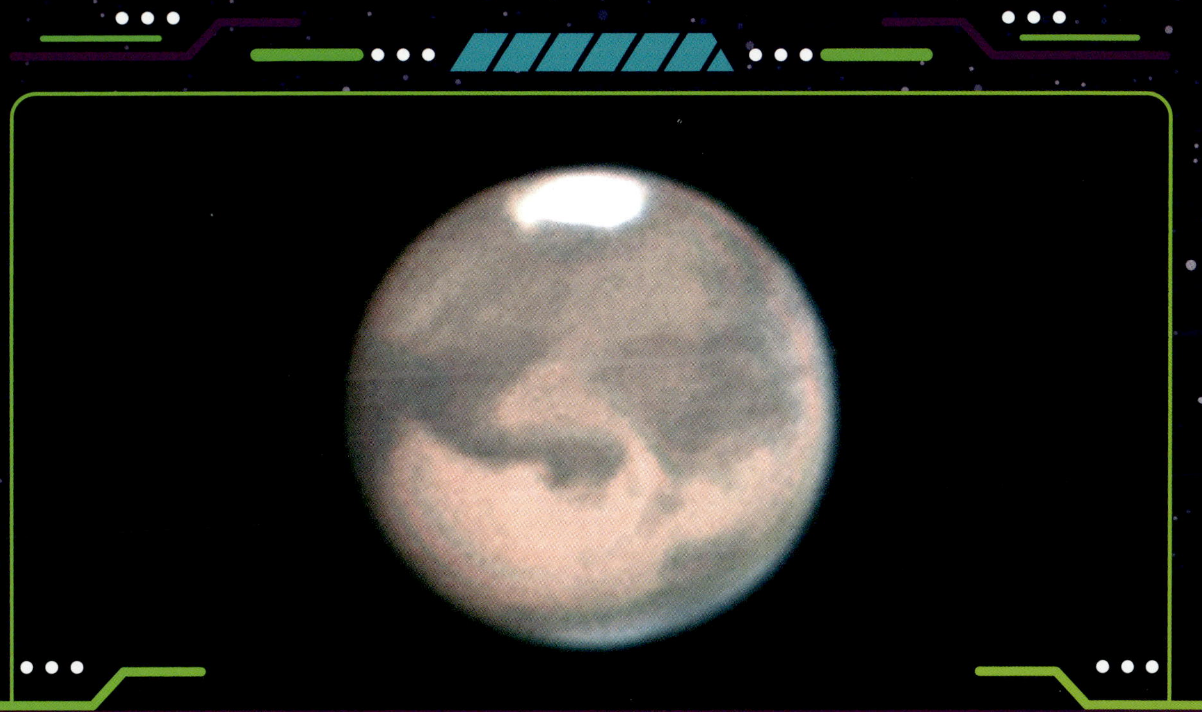

Early telescopes were not very powerful. Without clear details, it was easy for astronomers to imagine things that weren't there. For example, in 1784, a man named Sir William Herschel wrote that the dark patches on Mars were oceans and the light patches were solid ground. Today we know this isn't true.

SOJOURNER

From the 1960s onward, scientists began seriously trying to get a close look at Mars. About half of their missions failed. The other half rewarded humanity with pictures and **samples** from the planet as they flew by on their way to other parts of space. By the late 1990s, NASA was ready to put a machine on Mars that would stay there for years and return much more information than a flyby mission could.

On December 4, 1996, NASA sent a rocket to Mars containing a lander called *Pathfinder* and a rover called *Sojourner*. Although other spacecraft had landed on Mars in the past, *Sojourner* was the first Mars rover. *Pathfinder* and *Sojourner* were both loaded with instruments, or tools, to study and measure various things on Mars.

NASA KNOWLEDGE

A lander is a piece of equipment that is meant to stay in one place. A rover, in contrast, is meant to move around.

Shown here is a tiny model of the *Sojourner* rover.
The real thing was about 25 inches (64 cm) long,
19 inches (48 cm) wide, and 12 inches (30 cm) high.

MORE ROVERS

NASA expected *Sojourner* to work for only seven sols and to travel fewer than 72 feet (22 m). Instead, the little rover lived for 83 sols and covered at least 330 feet (100 m) around *Pathfinder*, which sent *Sojourner*'s discoveries back to Earth. The information NASA gained from *Sojourner* inspired scientists to make more rovers.

In 2004, NASA sent two rovers called *Spirit* and *Opportunity* to Mars. Next came *Curiosity* in 2012. Each of these rovers sent new information about the planet back to scientists on Earth. For example, by studying Mars's rocks, *Spirit* and *Opportunity* confirmed that Mars used to have liquid water on its surface. As of 2024, *Curiosity* is still active. *Spirit* stopped working in March 2010, and *Opportunity* stopped working in February 2019.

NASA KNOWLEDGE
A sol is one Mars day. It lasts for about 40 minutes longer than one day on Earth.

This model of *Opportunity* is on display in the Smithsonian National Air and Space Museum in Washington, D.C. *Opportunity*, nicknamed "Oppy" by NASA, was active on Mars for more than 14 years.

MISSION GOALS

The rovers are part of NASA's Mars Exploration Mission. This mission has four main goals:

- Learn whether there has ever been life on Mars.
- **Characterize** Mars's climate.
- Characterize Mars's geography.
- Prepare for a manned mission.

Information from the Mars rovers and **orbiters** has already helped scientists work toward these goals. For example, we now know that there is probably liquid water under the surface in a few places. There may also be large bodies of water under the ice at the planet's poles.

The instruments on the rovers have also provided information about the ground and air on Mars. From this information, scientists learned more about how seasons and weather work on Mars. They also now know more about how the current climate on Mars is different than it was in the distant past.

HUMANS ON MARS

Scientists hope to send people to Mars someday. The Mars rovers and orbiters are helping scientists gather information that will help them do this safely. The data gathered through photos and sample **analysis** will help NASA design spacesuits and living quarters that can withstand the conditions on Mars. Although they have already learned a lot, they still have much more to learn before any human can safely be sent to Mars.

The *Curiosity* rover took these pictures three days apart during a dust storm. They clearly show that the amount of dust in the air increased during that time.

PERSEVERANCE

Each time NASA sends a rover to Mars, they learn what works well on the rover and what needs to be improved. They can then make adjustments to the next rover so it performs its job even better than the old rovers did. Additionally, technology continues to advance over the years. Every time scientists make a new rover, they have access to better parts, instruments, and ways of doing things. For these reasons, *Perseverance* is the most advanced Mars rover so far.

About 85 percent of *Perseverance* is based on *Curiosity*. The body and some of the tools onboard are very similar. For example, *Perseverance* and *Curiosity* both have six wheels, one robotic arm, a drill for taking rock samples, and cameras.

NASA KNOWLEDGE

NASA gave *Perseverance* the nickname "Percy."

Curiosity took this selfie on Mars in 2021.

DIFFERENT TASKS

Because *Curiosity* and *Perseverance* were built for two different tasks, their onboard instruments are not the same. *Curiosity* was built to see if Mars could have sustained life in the past. Its instruments allow it to do things such as determine which chemicals are present in the dirt and rocks on Mars and in what amounts.

In contrast, *Perseverance*'s main goal is to look for direct evidence of ancient Martians, so that is what its instruments are made to help it do. For instance, one of *Perseverance*'s instruments is designed to detect any **organic** material that may be in Mars's rocks. Another instrument will let *Perseverance* drill directly into rock to take samples. NASA hopes to design future missions in a way that will let them bring those samples back to Earth for closer study.

MANY FORMS

When people think of aliens, they often think of humanoid, or humanlike, creatures that are as intelligent as humans. However, life comes in many forms. It's possible that in Mars's early days, when it had a thicker atmosphere and liquid water, life began to form. *Perseverance* is looking for evidence that this very early life existed. There is also a small possibility that bacteria live on Mars. The rock samples will help scientists see if this is the case.

Perseverance is studying the rocks on Mars. One of its 23 cameras took a picture of this avocado-shaped rock on September 8, 2023.

PREPARING FOR HUMANS

NASA is also using *Perseverance* to test some instruments that could help astronauts on a manned mission. One of these is called the Mars Oxygen In-Situ Resource Utilization Experiment (MOXIE). Mars's atmosphere is 95 percent carbon dioxide, which is the gas we breathe out on Earth. It is made up of one carbon atom and two oxygen atoms.

MOXIE separates one oxygen atom from each molecule of carbon dioxide the instrument takes in. This generates, or creates, pure oxygen. MOXIE is a small instrument, and it was included in *Perseverance* as a test of its abilities. Now that scientists know it works well, they can make a bigger **version** that could help give astronauts on Mars breathable air.

MOXIE is small, so it does not generate much oxygen. A bigger version would be able to take in more carbon dioxide at one time.

A FRIEND FOR PERCY

Perseverance did not go to Mars alone. A small helicopter called *Ingenuity* was strapped to the rover's belly. When *Perseverance* landed on the planet, it **deployed** *Ingenuity*. The helicopter made history on April 19, 2021, when it became the first aircraft to fly on another planet.

Ingenuity was mainly included in the mission as a technology test. NASA scientists now know that controlled flight on Mars is possible. The helicopter also took pictures of Mars from the air. Scientists used those pictures to plan where to send *Perseverance* next and to get a better sense of Mars's geography. Having completed these tasks, *Ingenuity* flew for the last time on January 18, 2024.

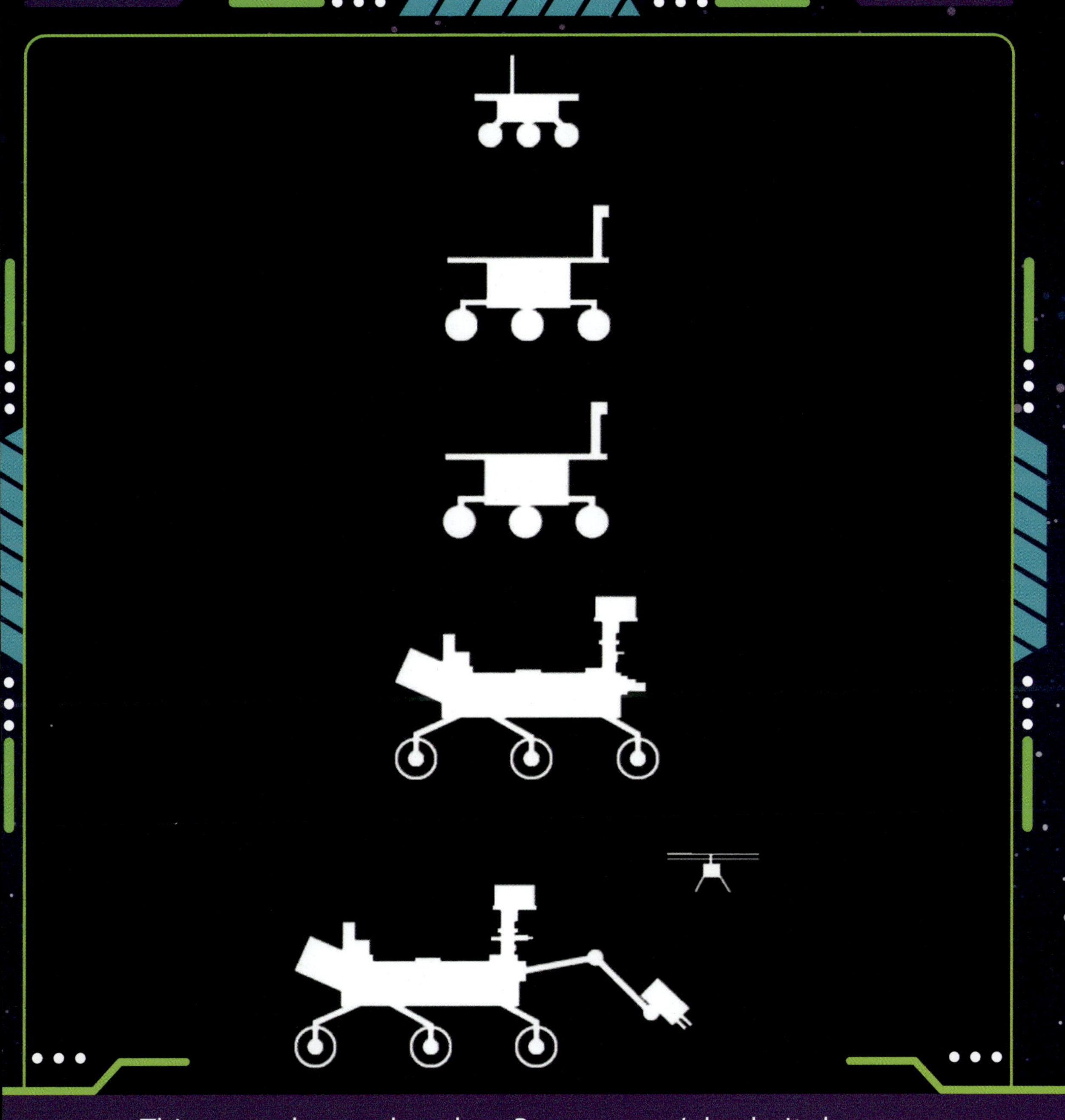

This artwork was placed on *Perseverance*'s body. It shows all the machines that have been sent to Mars, from *Sojourner* (top) to *Ingenuity* (bottom right).

No mission, no matter how carefully planned, goes perfectly. NASA scientists try to plan for every problem they can think of, but something unexpected always comes up. For *Perseverance*, this happened the first time it tried to drill into a rock.

Perseverance landed in Jezero Crater, which was named after a town in the country of Bosnia. When the rover tried to drill into one of the rocks in that crater, the rock crumbled to dust, so *Perseverance* was not able to get a good sample. The team controlling *Perseverance* moved the rover to a different part of the crater to try again. Luckily, these rocks were harder, and the samples were collected successfully.

ROCK CORE

NAMING MARS FEATURES

NASA names every feature the rovers find on Mars. This helps scientists keep track of what they're studying. In the earliest days of Mars exploration, scientists named features after cartoon characters. Today, there are more guidelines for names. For example, NASA's policy for craters is to name ones larger than 37 miles (60 km) after famous scientists or science-fiction authors. Any craters smaller than that are named after Earth towns with a population of less than 100,000.

After a small setback, *Perseverance* made history by collecting the first core samples from Mars rocks. The holes in this rock show where *Perseverance* drilled into it.

FINDINGS

Although it has only been on Mars for a short time, *Perseverance* has already made some exciting discoveries. Some confirmed what scientists already suspected, or guessed. Others gave them totally new information. For instance, studying photos from Mars orbiters made NASA scientists believe that Jezero Crater had once been a lake. They were not surprised when data from *Perseverance* confirmed this.

However, what did surprise NASA was *Perseverance's* finding that some of the rocks in the crater were igneous. This told scientists that the crater was filled with a lake of lava billions of years ago. Over time, the lava cooled to create the igneous rocks, and water flowed over them to create a shallow lake and salty mudflats. Scientists believe this could have been a good place for life to start forming.

A CHANGING LANDSCAPE

Mars's surface changed a lot over time. In Jezero Crater, the shallow lake eventually got deeper and then created a river. At some point, scientists believe this river flooded, carrying large rocks into the crater and depositing them there. Much later, when Mars lost most of its atmosphere, the water dried up. Scientists have learned about Mars's early landscape by studying the patterns flowing water left behind and comparing them to similar patterns on Earth.

A mudflat is a thick layer of **silt** and mud that is deposited by some bodies of water.

In addition to learning about Mars's ancient landscape, *Perseverance* may have made progress toward its main goal of finding evidence of ancient life. In July 2024, the rover found **mottling** known as "leopard spots" on a rock. On Earth, these spots form due to chemical reactions involving hematite, a mineral that has iron in it.

Scientists know that hematite is present on Mars. In fact, the rust from hematite is one of the things that makes the Martian soil red. The chemical reactions that cause leopard spots to form can be an energy source for **microbes**. While this is not definite proof that microbes once lived on Mars, it's a starting point for further research.

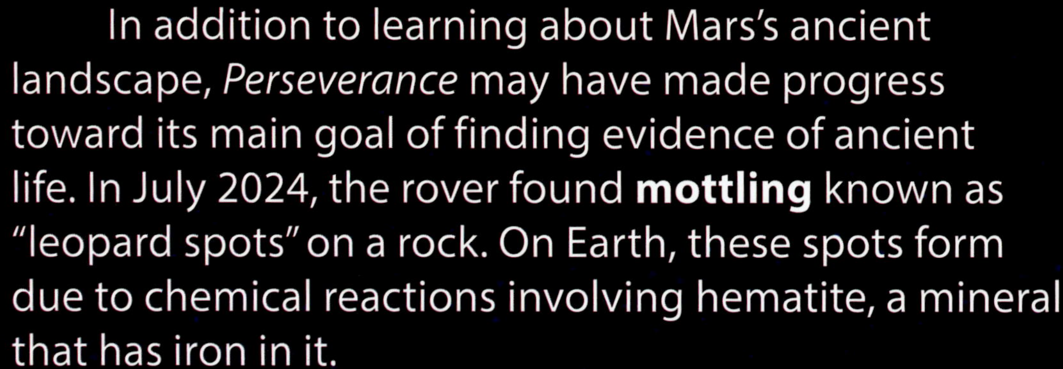

This picture shows the leopard spots
that *Perseverance* found on a Martian rock.

EXCEEDING EXPECTATIONS

Perseverance was designed to last at least one Mars year, or 687 Earth days. However, it's very likely the rover will keep going for many years after that. All the Mars rovers have lived much longer than NASA expected them to. *Spirit* and *Opportunity* were designed to last for three months, but *Spirit* lasted six years and *Opportunity* lasted nearly 15.

Spirit and *Opportunity* ran on solar power. This caused problems during dust storms, when their solar panels were covered with too much dust to soak up sunlight. *Perseverance*, however, is nuclear-powered. It will last as long as its fuel does. *Curiosity*, which is also nuclear-powered, has been running well for more than eight years. It's likely both rovers will last more than a decade.

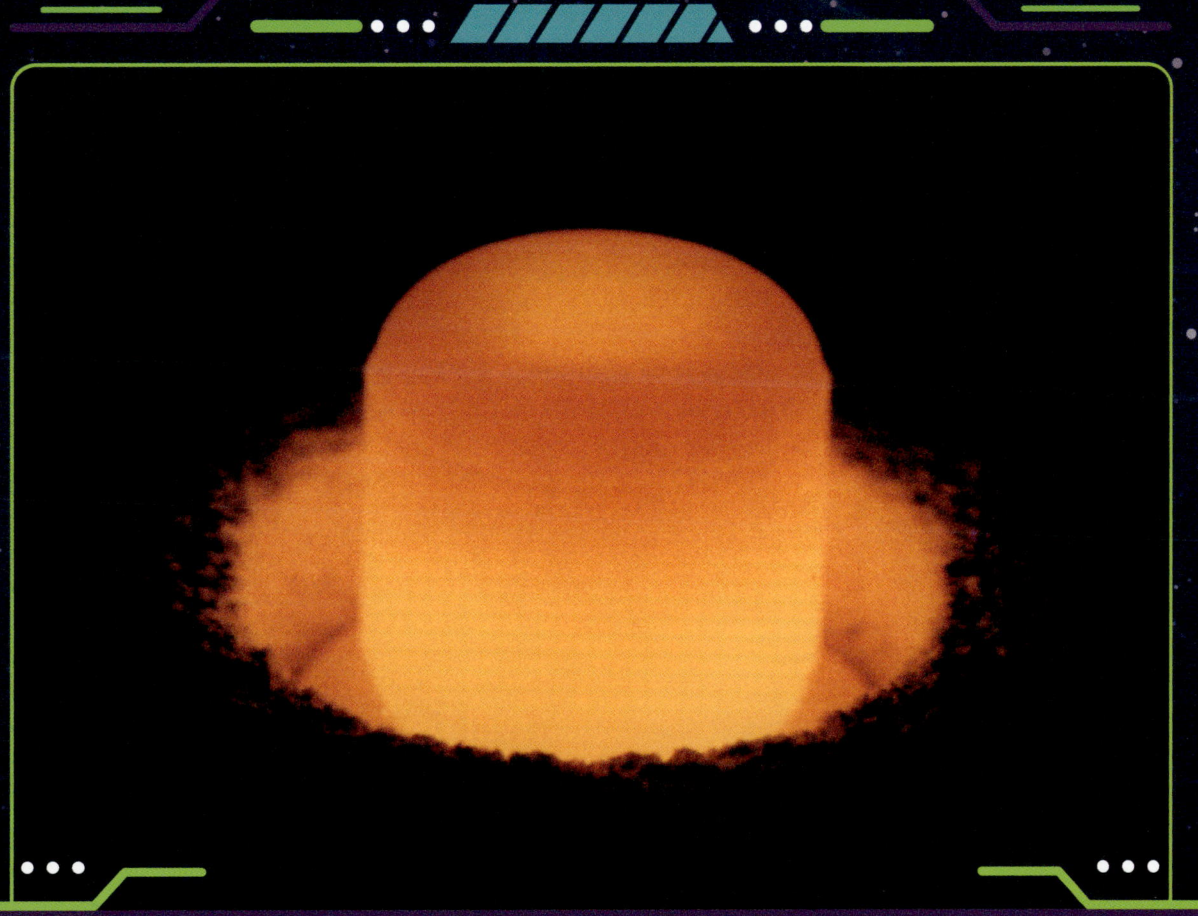

Perseverance is powered by plutonium-238. As this material decays, it gives off heat, which the MMRTG turns into energy.

THE FUTURE OF PERSEVERANCE

NASA will keep operating *Perseverance* as long as it can. The rover will keep collecting samples and photos to help scientists learn more about Mars. Although *Perseverance* will never return to Earth, it is collecting samples for a future mission to take home. On Earth, scientists have access to much better equipment than a rover would be able to carry into space. Studying *Perseverance*'s samples will help NASA learn even more about Mars.

Perseverance has already taught us many new things about Mars. It will continue to do so for many years to come. Its best features will be added to new rovers, and scientists will study any problems it has to make future rovers better.

A coded message on the parachute that dropped *Perseverance* safely on Mars's surface spelled out "Dare mighty things."

GLOSSARY

analysis: The process of analyzing something, or studying it deeply.

canal: A man-made waterway.

characterize: To describe the qualities that make up someone or something.

deploy: To move, spread out, or place in position for some purpose.

microbe: A very small living thing that can only be seen with a microscope.

mottling: Colored spots or blotches on a surface.

orbiter: A spacecraft that orbits a heavenly body but does not land on it.

organic: Of, relating to, or obtained from living things.

sample: A part that represents the whole.

silt: Very small particles left as sediment from water.

version: A form of something that is different than the ones that came before it.